POLAR ANIMALS

Wade Cooper

Cartwheel
B·O·O·K·S®

SCHOLASTIC INC.

New York Toronto London Auckland Sydney
Mexico City New Delhi Hong Kong Buenos Aires

Could you live in the snow,
on the ice, sharp and bright?
Would you shiver? Would you shake?
Do you love the color white?

Bundle up and come with us
and then you'll understand
more about the animals
who love this frozen land.

ISBN-13: 978-0-545-00718-4
ISBN-10: 0-545-00718-6
10 9 8 7 6 5 4 3 2 1   7 8 9 10 11
Printed in China
First printing, September 2007

Reading together

This book is an ideal first reader for your child, combining simple words and sentences with stunning color photography of real-life animals. Here are some of the many ways you can help your child take those first steps in reading. Encourage your child to:

- Look at and explore the detail in the pictures.

- Sound out the letters in each word.

- Read and repeat each short sentence.

Look at the pictures

Make the most of each page by talking about the pictures and spotting key words. Here are some questions you can use to discuss each page as you go along:

- Why do you like this animal?

- What would it feel like to touch?

- How does it keep itself warm?

- What noise does it make?

- Do you like the snow and ice?

Look at rhymes

Some of the sentences in this book are simple rhymes. Encourage your child to recognize rhyming words. Try asking the following questions:

- What does this word say?

- Can you find a word that rhymes with it?

- Look at the ending of two words that rhyme. Are they spelled the same? For example, "long" and "strong," and "meat" and "feet."

Test understanding

It is one thing to understand the meaning of individual words, but you need to check that your child understands the facts in the text.

- Play "spot the obvious mistake." Read the text as your child looks at the words with you, but make an obvious mistake to see if he or she has understood. Ask your child to correct you and provide the right word.

- After reading the facts, shut the book and make up questions to ask your child.

- Ask your child whether a fact is true or false.

- Provide your child with three answers to a question and ask him or her to pick the correct one.

Quiz pages

At the end of the book there is a simple quiz. Ask the questions and see if your child can remember the right answers from the text. If not, encourage him or her to look up the answers.

Polar animals

The North Pole and South Pole
are the coldest places on Earth.

North Pole

South Pole

Animals that live in snow and ice need to keep warm. Some have thick fur. Some have fluffy feathers. Some are big and fat.

Lots of polar animals are white so they can hide in the snow.

I'm large.
I'm long.
I'm very strong.

I look very cuddly
with my furry feet.
But I get hungry
when I smell fresh meat.

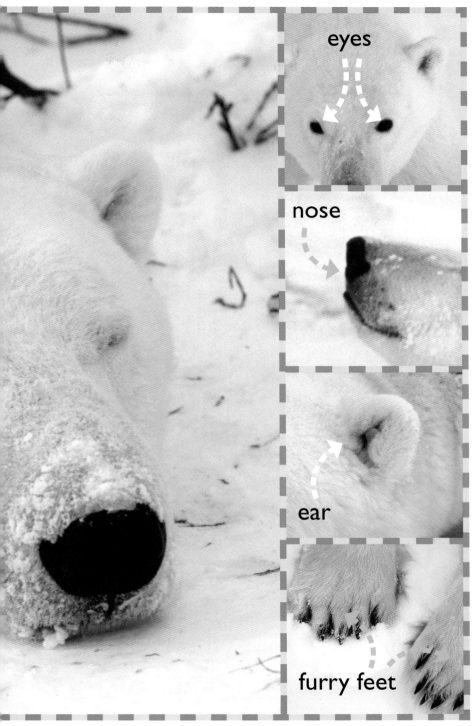

eyes

nose

ear

furry feet

11

Yes, I'm a polar bear.
I'm hairy.
I'm scary.
Beware!

Grrrrr

I have whiskers and tusks.
I am wrinkly and fat.

I can sleep in the water.
And that is that!

big eyes

sharp beak

talons

I'm a snowy owl.
I live in the ground.
I fly over grasslands.
I don't make a sound.

hoohooo
hoohooo

In winter,
my fur is thick and white.

It keeps me very warm.

In summer,
my fur turns gray and brown.

I can hide
and be safe from harm.

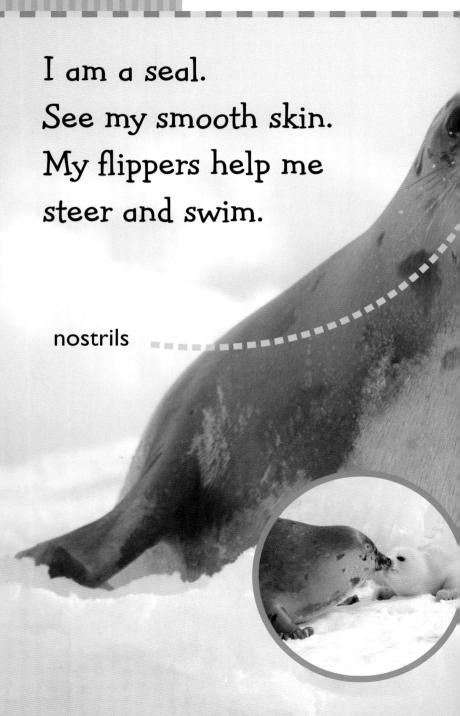

I am a seal.
See my smooth skin.
My flippers help me
steer and swim.

nostrils

whiskers

flipper

I make a hole in the ice to catch fish to eat.

I jump in the water
when I hear bear feet.

Penguin

We're black-and-white penguins

We're birds who cannot fly.

Penguin

feet

flipper

tail

beak

wheeeee

We can leap and dive.
We can swim and slide.

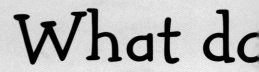

What do

1. What do polar bears eat?

They eat fresh meat.

2. Which polar animal has whiskers and tusks?

A walrus

3. Where do snowy owls live?

In a hole in the ground

you know?

4. Can a penguin fly?

No. It uses its wings for swimming.

5. What does a seal use its flippers for?

For steering and swimming underwater

6. What color is an arctic fox in summer?

Gray and brown

Useful words

tusk
A tusk is a long, pointed tooth.
A walrus has two tusks.

whisker
Whiskers are the long hairs
on an animal's face.

feather
All birds have feathers to
keep them warm and dry.

flipper
A seal's flippers are its arms.
Seals use their flippers
for swimming.

wrinkly
Skin that is wrinkly is
covered in lines. A walrus
has wrinkly skin.